Machu Picchu

UNEARTHING ANCIENT WORLDS

Deborah Kops

Twenty-First Century Books • Minneapolis

For John and Noah, with love

Twenty-First Century Books
A division of Lerner Publishing Group, Inc.
241 First Avenue North
Minneapolis, MN 55401 U.S.A.

Website address: www.lernerbooks.com

Library of Congress Cataloging-in-Publication Data

Kops, Deborah.
    Machu Picchu / by Deborah Kops.
       p.   cm. — (Unearthing ancient worlds)
    Includes bibliographical references and index.
    ISBN 978–0–8225–7584–9 (lib. bdg. : alk. paper)
    1. Machu Picchu Site (Peru)—Juvenile literature. 2. Incas—History—Juvenile literature. 3. Inca architecture—Juvenile literature. 4. Peru—Antiquities—Juvenile literature. I. Title.
F3429.1.M3K66 2009
985'.37—dc22   2007052618

Manufactured in the United States of America
1 2 3 4 5 6 – PA – 14 13 12 11 10 09

TABLE OF CONTENTS

The sun rises over Machu Picchu in the Andes Mountains in Peru. The ancient city is located between two mountain peaks and is surrounded by tree-covered slopes.

INTRODUCTION

In the A.D. 1400s, a group of people called the Inca built the small city of Machu Picchu. The city lay northwest of Cuzco, the capital of the great Inca Empire. Machu Picchu stood on a ridge between two peaks in the Andes Mountains of Peru in South America. The ridge rose steeply above tree-covered mountain slopes and the rushing Urubamba River. The builders placed two large temples near the top of the ridge. The site was one of the finest spots in Machu Picchu. From there the Inca enjoyed the beautiful scenery. On clear days, they looked up at the blue sky. And they peered down at the roaring river below.

Inca farmers carved the slopes around Machu Picchu into terraces for growing crops.

Examples of the Inca's skills as engineers and builders lay everywhere in Machu Picchu. On one side of the ridge, the Inca found a way to farm the sloping land. They carved it into terraces. These flat areas looked like giant steps covered with soil. Farmers cultivated corn, beans, and potatoes for the residents of Machu Picchu.

On the other section of the ridge, the Inca

This house at Machu Picchu has been reconstructed to look like it did originally. It has a high sloping roof.

lived in simple stone houses. Their windows and doorways framed views of distant mountain peaks. Engineers designed fountains to provide residents with water for drinking and bathing. The water came from natural springs. Workers dug channels to direct the spring water to the fountains.

The Inca people worshipped many gods, including sun and moon gods. They also believed that rocks and mountains were sacred. Stonemasons at Machu Picchu carved some of the large rocks jutting out of the ground into a variety of shapes. Inside the Temple of the Sun, they carved a rock formation to look like a wild cat. It was probably a puma—an animal that was sacred to the Inca.

A man named Pachacuti headed the Inca Empire from 1438 to 1471. Experts think that the Inca built Machu Picchu during Pachacuti's reign. Pachacuti liked to wear puma skins when he went to war. Under his leadership, the Inca Empire expanded to about two-thirds of its final size.

FAST FACTS

- The Inca Empire lasted less than two centuries. It began as a small kingdom during the 1300s and ended in 1572.
- The empire became much larger when Pachacuti ruled the Inca. He ruled from 1438 to 1471.
- The empire eventually stretched across 2,400 miles (4,000 kilometers) of modern Peru and Ecuador, as well as large parts of Chile, Bolivia, and Argentina. It included more than ten million people.
- The Inca built Machu Picchu in the 1400s.
- The Inca had deserted Machu Picchu by the time the empire ended in 1572.

Eventually, the empire occupied all of modern Peru and Ecuador. It also stretched across large sections of Chile, Bolivia, and Argentina. It spanned about 2,400 miles (4,000 km). More than ten million people lived in the empire.

The Inca Empire was still
growing in 1532. But at the
end of that year, everything
changed. The Spanish
conqueror Francisco Pizarro
arrived in the Andes Mountains in Peru. On November 16, he and his
soldiers captured the ruler of the Inca Empire. Eventually they killed him.
The Spanish allowed another member of the royal family to be the ruler.
His name was Manco. The Spanish thought they could control Manco. With
his help, they believed, they would crush the Inca people.

Eventually the Spanish conquerors seized most of the land that
belonged to the Inca. But the Inca did not give up their independence
completely. Manco escaped from the Spanish in Cuzco. He moved his
kingdom to the wilderness about 125 miles (200 km) away. For thirty-six
years, Manco and his descendants governed from a series of new cities.
The rulers sent soldiers to fight the Spanish. They hoped to get back the
land they had lost. Finally, in 1572, the Spanish captured and executed the

last Inca ruler, Tupac Amarú. His death ended the Inca's final struggle for independence. The Inca Empire had reached its end.

By 1572 the Inca had deserted Machu Picchu. They no longer strolled past the fountains, enjoying the sound of trickling water. No one worshipped in the Temple of the Sun. And no one admired the views of tall mountain peaks hidden in the clouds.

The Spanish ruled Peru for almost three hundred years. During that time, people hunting for gold destroyed old Inca buildings. The Spanish used some of the remaining walls to construct churches and palaces. But the Spanish probably never visited Machu Picchu. That beautiful city lay undisturbed for four centuries. Eventually, only a few local people knew that Machu Picchu existed.

Modern scholars are not sure whether the Inca had a written form of communication. If the Inca left any written accounts about Machu Picchu, no one has found them yet. Why did the Inca build that magical place? What exactly did they do there?

The Andes Mountains rise behind fields in the Urubamba Valley in Peru. Hiram Bingham and his team traveled to the Urubamba River area in 1911.

CHAPTER one

HIRAM BINGHAM'S EXPEDITION TO PERU

Hiram Bingham III seems to have it all. This tall and handsome man lives with his wife and six sons in a thirty-room mansion. He teaches the history of South America at Yale University in New Haven, Connecticut. He had gone to college there. Yale is one of the finest educational institutions in the United States.

But Bingham does not like spending months at a time in a classroom. Instead of teaching college students about South America, he would much rather explore it.

In 1911 Bingham begins organizing his third trip to South America in five years. He wants to see the ruins of old Inca cities.

Hiram Bingham III, shown in a photograph from 1924, was fascinated by unexplored Inca cities. He made many trips to South America to find ancient ruins.

On his last trip to Peru, Bingham had visited some Inca ruins in the Andes Mountains. They were mainly poorly built houses in bad condition. To reach the ruins, he and his companion had followed a muddy, slippery trail through the wilderness. It was during the rainiest season in Peru. They had crossed a river on a suspension bridge made of rope. The bridge dangled hundreds of feet above the rushing water. Bingham loved the grand mountain scenery surrounding the ruins. And he actually enjoyed the dangerous journey to reach them. Bingham hopes to find more Inca ruins on this next trip.

Bingham is not an archaeologist—an expert who studies old buildings, graves, tools, and other artifacts (objects) to learn about old cultures and civilizations. Very few archaeologists at this time have explored the remains of Inca settlements. Most prefer to study the ruins of ancient Greece and the Middle East. But Bingham is an experienced explorer. And he does know South American history.

The Yale professor wants to find the cities in Peru where the Inca rulers and their followers lived after the Spanish conquered Cuzco. Bingham also hopes to make a different sort of discovery in Peru. He plans to be the first person to climb Mount Coropuna. This extinct volcano lies in the Andes Mountains in the southern part

Hiram Bingham wanted to climb Mount Coropuna (below) on his 1911 expedition to Peru.

of the country. Bingham has read that the mountain may be the tallest in South America. Since no one has climbed Coropuna, no one knows exactly how high it is. The tallest peaks in the Andes are more than 20,000 feet (6,100 meters) above sea level.

Mount Coropuna is south of the Inca ruins Bingham saw on his last trip. When Bingham looks at a map, he notices something interesting. Both the mountain and the ruins are near the 73rd meridian in southern Peru. A meridian is an imaginary circle around Earth that runs through the North and South poles.

Bingham decides to explore part of the wilderness along the 73rd meridian. In Peru the meridian runs from the Andes to the Pacific Ocean. Bingham wants to map the land along the meridian. In the process, maybe he will find the cities where the last Inca rulers lived.

WANTED: A GROUP OF EXPLORERS

Bingham needs people who can help him achieve his goals. For example, he wants a professional topographer. The topographer will measure and map the physical features of the land along the 73rd meridian. And he would like an experienced mountain climber to hike Mount Coropuna with him.

The Yale professor manages to find six capable men to join him. Kai Hendriksen is a topographer from Denmark. In fact, he is Denmark's royal chief surveyor. He helped the U.S. government survey the border between the state of Maine and the nation of Canada to the north. Herman Tucker is an experienced mountain climber.

The other four men have connections with Yale University. Harry Foote is a professor of chemistry there. He is also a friend of Bingham's. Foote has done a lot of camping in the wilderness. He has never traveled to Peru, however. Foote is excited about the unusual birds, insects, and wildflowers he expects to see.

Isaiah Bowman is a professor of geography at Yale. He has already been to southern Peru to study the region's geography. Dr. William Erving is a college friend of Bingham's. Erving is a medical doctor. Like Bingham, he loves exploring. Erving has paddled a canoe on the Nile River in northern Africa for more than 1,000 miles (1,600 km).

Hiram Bingham stands inside one of the tents in camp on the trip to Peru in 1911.

"To be sure . . . some of the younger men may feel that their reputations as explorers are likely to be damaged if it is known that strawberry jam, sweet chocolate and pickles are frequently found on the menu!"

—Hiram Bingham, 1922

Paul Lanius was once a student of Bingham's. He knows Spanish, the most widely used language in South America, and has lived in Peru. He is only twenty-one years old and will assist the other members of the expedition. Bingham, the expedition's leader, is thirty-five.

Bingham has plenty of experienced help for his trip. He persuades Yale University to lend its famous name to the expedition. It becomes known as the Yale Peruvian Expedition.

Foote helps Bingham organize supplies. They assemble twenty boxes of food for their travels in Peru. The boxes contain crushed oats and coffee for breakfast, canned meats for dinner, and chocolate for a treat. The boxes of food will come in handy when the expedition cannot buy fresh meat and vegetables in Peru. Bingham and Foote also pack folding cots, blankets, and tents. They believe that explorers do not need to rough it to prove they are adventurous. Even in the wilderness, they can eat well and be fairly comfortable most of the time.

THE EXPEDITION STEAMS AHEAD

In April 1911, Annie Peck, a female explorer and mountain climber, reads about Bingham's plans to climb Mount Coropuna. She has already climbed a mountain in Peru that she claimed was the highest in South America. Annie Peck decides that she will climb Mount Coropuna too. Bingham is afraid she plans to get there first.

Bingham has already decided to climb Mount Coropuna at the end of the expedition. This large mountain has several peaks. He hopes that Peck will make a mistake and climb one of the shorter peaks.

On May 25, 1911, Dr. William Erving and Kai Hendriksen leave New York City for South America on board a steamship. The doctor and topographer take most of the expedition's supplies and equipment with them. Bingham has asked them to find about twenty mules when they arrive in Peru. The men will depend on mules for transportation. Mules will also carry the supplies and equipment. The rest of the expedition team plans to meet with Erving and Hendriksen in Cuzco.

On June 8, Bingham and the other four expedition members leave. But Bingham switches to a different ship in Panama in Central America. He has learned that Annie Peck is on that boat. Maybe he wants to see his competitor up close. On the long voyage to Lima, the capital of Peru, they do not speak to each other once. Bingham does notice that she is not a young woman. In fact, the mountain climber is more than sixty years old.

IN LIMA

In Lima Bingham has to wait three days for his companions to arrive. He does not like to waste time. And he is not shy. So he pays a visit to Augusto Leguía, the president of Peru. Bingham has met the president once before. He tells the president about the Yale Peruvian Expedition. The goals of the expedition impress Leguía. He offers Bingham a military escort. A military officer and soldiers will accompany the expedition on its travels. Bingham happily accepts the offer.

Foote, Bowman, Tucker, and Lanius finally arrive in Lima. Together with Bingham, they take a boat to a town on the coast of southern Peru.

From there the men take a four-day train ride to Cuzco. They will join Erving and Hendriksen, who are already there.

When the train is just one stop away from Cuzco, two familiar faces suddenly appear. Erving and Hendriksen have gotten on the train. They want the pleasure of riding with their five friends for the last lap of their long journey. At last all seven members of the expedition are together.

Cuzco lies in a valley of the Andes Mountains. It was once the capital of the Inca Empire. In fact, many of the native peoples who live in Cuzco are descendants of the Inca. Bingham calls the native peoples Indians. They speak Quechua, the language of the Inca.

BINGHAM FINDS SOME BONES

On July 9, Bingham notices a bone sticking out of a gravel bank near Cuzco. He becomes very excited. He shows the bone to Foote and Bowman.

Bowman and Foote take photos of the bone. Together the three men carefully excavate (dig) to remove it. They find more bones, and they photograph and remove them. Then the men match the pieces of bone into partial skeletons. They guess that they have found at least two humans and one animal.

Bowman studies the gravel bank. He thinks that glaciers deposited the gravel about thirty thousand years ago. (These large masses of ice move very slowly and can drag gravel and even big boulders.) The geographer concludes that the bones are about the same age. He thinks the animal bones may belong to an ancient bison. If Bowman is right, Bingham has

Hiram Bingham took this photograph of the bones he found near Cuzco. He sent the bones to the Peabody Museum at Yale University in Connecticut for further study.

made a very exciting discovery. He may have proved that humans arrived in South America thirty thousand years ago. In the early 1900s, most scholars believe that humans arrived in the Americas only about ten thousand years ago.

The men wrap the bones carefully in cotton. They ship them to the Peabody Museum of Natural History at Yale University. At the museum, a specialist will examine them.

A TIP ABOUT SOME INCA RUINS

While Bingham is in Cuzco, he meets the rector (head) of the local university. The rector tells Bingham about a recent trip he has taken on horseback. He was riding down a road northwest of Cuzco. The road is in a canyon along the Urubamba River. He stopped to rest at a tavern near a bridge. The tavern owner told the rector about some Inca ruins on the cliffs above the bridge. It sounds like a good tip to Bingham. He decides to see the ruins on the cliffs right away. First, though, he has to give every expedition member a task.

Hiram Bingham and his team followed the Urubamba River as they searched for Inca ruins. In this modern image, the Inca Trail is shown on the right. Some tourists use the

CHAPTER two

THE MYSTERIOUS WITCHERY OF THE JUNGLE

Hiram Bingham has three main goals for the Yale Peruvian Expedition. He wants to find the cities where the last Inca rulers lived. He would like his expedition members to survey some of the wilderness that lies along the 73rd meridian. Finally, Bingham plans to climb Mount Coropuna. He hopes to prove that the mountain is the highest in South America. (And if Annie Peck does get there first, Bingham hopes she won't make it to the summit.)

Bingham divides the men into groups. He asks Harry Foote to help him find the ruins of Inca cities. The remaining five men separate into two groups. Each group will survey a different part of the land along the 73rd meridian. Later, Bingham and Tucker will hike up Mount Coropuna. Everyone plans to take photographs of discoveries.

Some local men join the explorers. Mule drivers take charge of the animals that will carry the supplies. The president of Peru had promised to give Bingham a military escort. Three military men join the expedition. One soldier will accompany each of the groups that will survey the 73rd meridian in southern Peru. An army officer will accompany Bingham and Foote. He is Sergeant Carrasco.

THE CANYON OF THE URUBAMBA

On July 19, 1911, the three groups of explorers leave Cuzco. In Bingham's group, Bingham, Foote, and Carrasco ride on mules. Another eight mules follow with supplies. Two mule drivers and two helpers accompany them.

Bingham wants to follow up on the tip that the rector has given him. He wants to find the tavern owner who knows about some ruins above the cliffs. Bingham's group heads northwest along the Urubamba River. They descend to the floor of a canyon. The air is warmer there than it was in Cuzco. And the vegetation is much greener.

"It was in July, 1911, that we first entered that marvelous canyon of the Urubamba, where the river escapes from the cold regions near Cuzco by tearing its way through gigantic mountains of granite. . . . In the variety of its charms and the power of its spell, I know of no place in the world which can compare with it. Not only has it great snow peaks looming above the clouds more than two miles [3 km] overhead; gigantic precipices of many-colored granite rising sheer for thousands of feet above the foaming, glistening, roaring rapids; it has also, in striking contrast, orchids and tree ferns, the delectable beauty of luxurious vegetation, and the mysterious witchery of the jungle."

—Hiram Bingham, 1922

On July 23, Bingham finds the tavern near the bridge. The tavern is a simple hut with a grass roof. Bingham and his group set up camp on a sandy beach near the river. Carrasco tells the tavern owner they are looking for Inca ruins. The tavern owner describes the ruins on a nearby

Clouds fill the Urubamba River valley in Peru. Bingham and his team hiked in the valley as they looked for Inca ruins.

ridge called Machu Picchu. The ruins are near some land that he owns. Bingham hopes the tavern owner will take him there in the morning.

THE HIKE TO THE RIDGE

When the men wake up in the morning, they feel a chill in the damp air. It is drizzling outside. Shivering, the tavern owner tells Bingham that he will

Who's Who on the 1911 Expedition

Hiram Bingham	expedition leader
Isaiah Bowman	geographer
William Erving	medical doctor
Harry Foote	chemistry professor and wildlife expert
Kai Hendriksen	topographer
Paul Lanius	assistant
Herman Tucker	mountain climber

Hiram Bingham took this photo of the tavern owner crossing the Urubamba River. The bridge is made of only a few logs tied together.

not take him to the ruins on such a wet day. They will find it too difficult to climb up to the ridge. Bingham does not give up easily. He offers a generous payment in Peruvian money. So the tavern owner agrees to take him.

Carrasco accompanies Bingham and the tavern owner. Foote decides to stay near the river and look for butterflies he has never seen before.

The three men head down the road. They soon pass a dead yellow viper. It's a good thing the snake is dead because it is very poisonous. Bingham and his companions walk for less than an hour. Then they plunge through the thick jungle growth to reach the banks of the Urubamba River.

Bingham looks at the crude bridge they must cross. It is just a few slim logs. Some of them have been tied together with vines. Below the bridge rushes the foaming water of the Urubamba River. The tavern owner and the sergeant take off their shoes. They can grip the logs better with their toes. They walk across the bridge

"It was obvious that no one could have lived for an instant in the rapids, but would immediately have been dashed to pieces against granite boulders. I am frank to confess that I got down on hands and knees and crawled across, six inches [15 centimeters] at a time."

—Hiram Bingham, 1922

without falling in the water. Bingham, the bold explorer, is not feeling courageous. He prefers to crawl.

The men soon leave the river and climb a steep slope. They climb for almost an hour and a half. At times the slope is covered with grass, which they check for snakes. At other times, they climb over rock. Occasionally, they find a crude ladder carved into a tree trunk. The men become sweaty and uncomfortable as the day grows hot.

By early afternoon, Bingham, the sergeant, and the tavern owner reach a small grass-covered hut. The family living there seems pleasantly surprised to see them. They know the tavern owner because they rent their land from him. But they have never seen a tall American man before. Family members fill the shells of gourds with cool water for the travelers. Then the family serves them cooked sweet potatoes.

The family does not speak Spanish, which is the most common language in Peru. They speak Quechua. Carrasco knows the language. He asks the family about the ruins on the ridge. They reply that the ruins are nearby.

Bingham does not rush. He enjoys the view of the steep canyon below. And he can see some terraces that the Inca probably farmed hundreds of years ago.

Terraces: A Practical and Beautiful Solution

It is very difficult to farm land that slopes steeply. The Inca created terraces so that they would have flat surfaces to farm. These terraces had another advantage: They helped keep the soil from washing downhill after heavy rains. The Inca appreciated beauty as well as practicality. So they designed the terraces with great care.

Tourists walk around the ruins at Machu Picchu in this modern photograph. Because the city is high in the mountains, it is often surrounded by clouds.

CHAPTER three

THE SMALL CITY IN THE CLOUDS

When Bingham is finally ready to visit the ruins, a boy from the family living nearby agrees to take him there. Carrasco comes along, but the tavern owner stays behind with the family. The boy and two men make an interesting trio. The sergeant wears his uniform jacket with brass buttons. Bingham wears a shapeless green hat and casual clothing. The boy outshines them both. He wears a brightly colored poncho and a large hat. Shiny decorations dangle from the brim.

The three climb up the terraces that Bingham noticed from the hut. He admires their construction. Each one is about 200 yards (183 m) long and 10 feet (3 m) high. Bingham guesses that the family or their neighbors on the ridge have cleared the terraces recently.

The boy takes the two men into a big patch of jungle trees and bamboo. Suddenly, Bingham sees a maze of small houses made with granite blocks. Moss covers the stone. Trees and stalks of bamboo crowd around the buildings.

Bingham notices a white structure shaped like a half circle. He guesses this is a temple or tower with a curved wall. The wall amazes Bingham. The people who built it fitted together blocks of white granite very carefully. They did not use any mortar to keep them in place. And they did not have even the simplest tools that modern builders use to cut stones with straight edges. Bingham thinks the blocks fit together so perfectly that they seem to have grown together!

The boy takes Bingham up a long stairway to see two large buildings. Bingham guesses that these were temples. Each of them has only three walls, which are made of granite blocks. The open side of each temple faces a clearing.

Bingham calls one of the structures the Principal Temple. The other has a striking feature: three large windows. Bingham calls it the Temple of the Three Windows. Each one is about 3 feet (0.9 m) wide, 4 feet (1.2 m) high, and almost 3 feet (0.9 m) deep.

A view of the Andes Mountains behind the Temple of the Three Windows

"Surprise followed surprise in bewildering succession. I climbed a marvelous great stairway of large granite blocks, walked along a pampa [grassy plain] where the Indians had a small vegetable garden, and came into a little clearing. Here were the ruins of two of the finest structures I have ever seen in Peru. Not only were they made of selected blocks of beautifully grained white granite; their walls contained [blocks] . . . ten feet [3 m] in length and higher than a man. The sight held me spellbound."

—Hiram Bingham, 1922

The three walls of the Principal Temple (center) are visible in this modern photograph of Machu Picchu.

Bingham takes out his camera and shoots a lot of pictures. He climbs on top of a wall to take some more. He has a good view of Machu Picchu Mountain rising 2,000 feet (610 m) above him. When he hops down, he notices something else.

In the middle of a corn patch that one of the local families has planted near the wall, Bingham sees a large rock. Centuries ago, stoneworkers carved the top of the rock into a square column 20 inches (50 cm) high. Bingham guesses it's a type of sundial. He thinks the Inca probably used it to worship the sun. He asks the sergeant and the boy to stand near it and takes more pictures.

Bingham is surprised that only a few local people know about the ruins of Machu Picchu. After all, it takes only about five days to reach them from Cuzco. One reason may be that the road Bingham traveled along the Urubamba River is only about twenty years old. Before 1890 it would have been far more difficult to reach the ruins.

Did the Spanish conquerors know about this place? Bingham doubts this. He is familiar with many documents from the 1500s, when the Spanish conquered the Inca.

Hiram Bingham took this photograph of Sergeant Carrasco and their young guide standing next to the sundial.

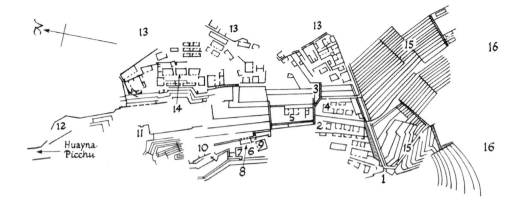

MACHU PICCHU (after Bingham's plan, first published in 1913)

13   13   13   15   16

14   3   15   16

12

Huayna
Picchu   11   5   2

10   7 6 9   15

8   1

1. City Gate   2. divided stairway and round tower over first cave   3. Stairway of the Fountains
4. Royal Mausoleum   5. King's Group   6. Sacred Plaza   7. Principal Temple
8. Temple of the Three Windows   9. High Priest's house   10. Intihuatana Hill   11. terraced gardens
12. terraced gardens and sacrificial rocks   13. main residential areas, with terraces and burial caves below
14. Three-Door Group   15. agricultural terraces   16. steep hillsides covered with rubble, probably former
    agricultural terraces

Hiram Bingham drew this map
of the ruins at Machu Picchu.
The map was first published
in 1913.

Some soldiers, priests, and other
Spanish people in Peru tried to learn all
they could about the Inca. Many of these
records survived. Scholars call them the
Spanish chronicles. Bingham has found
no mention in the Spanish chronicles of an Inca settlement at Machu Picchu.

The expedition leader sketches a map of all he has seen. Then he is
ready to return to the hut with the boy and Carrasco. He wants to get the
tavern owner and leave. Bingham is anxious to reach the campsite by the
Urubamba River before dark.

IN SEARCH OF LOST CITIES

Hiram Bingham knows he may have made an important discovery. But
he does not spend a lot of time thinking about it. There is still much
to explore. Bingham wants to search for the cities where the last Inca
rulers lived. The Spanish chronicles mention two in particular: Vitcos and
Vilcabamba. The author of one of the chronicles describes Vitcos as a
fortress with a view of the land surrounding the Vilcabamba River.

Bingham, Foote, and the sergeant leave the next day to look for the two lost cities. First, they head north up the Urubamba River. Bingham asks local people about nearby ruins. No one seems to know of any. The explorers turn back and travel south until they reach the Vilcabamba River. Bingham believes they may have better luck in the Vilcabamba River valley. He is right.

In a small village, a local official knows about some ruins. Once again, Bingham offers a generous payment. He asks the official to show him the ruins. The official takes Bingham to a hill in a nearby village. The men begin to climb. When they are halfway up the hill, Bingham sees the ruins of a large stone building about 166 feet (50 m) long. He guesses it was a military barracks—housing for soldiers. At the top of the hill, the explorer sees a group of stone houses surrounded by a wall. There is also a white granite building larger than any at Machu Picchu. Bingham concludes that this is the fortress described in the Spanish chronicles. He has found Vitcos only two weeks after seeing Machu Picchu.

VILCABAMBA

In a nearby village, Bingham learns about the ruins of Vilcabamba. The ruins are northwest of Vitcos. A local official warns that they will have to leave their mules behind. The road through the wilderness is too rough for the animals.

A day or two later, Bingham, Foote, and Carrasco are on their way. They hike 50 miles (80 km) downhill and descend 9,000 feet (2,743 m)! They soon find themselves in a steamy hot rain forest in a river valley.

The owner of a small sugarcane plantation tells Bingham about some ruins in the woods. They may be the ruins of the old Inca city of Vilcabamba. He sends some workers to help Bingham clear away trees so he can measure the buildings.

Bingham finds the ruins of a good-sized settlement hidden by thick vegetation. He and his helpers work for two days to clear away the trees and shrubs. They uncover houses, terraces, and stairways. The foundation for one large building is about 200 feet (61 m) long. The structures are not as well made as the ones at Machu Picchu. Bingham notices tiles that

Hiram Bingham *(far left)* and others stand at Vilcabamba, the third Inca ruins Bingham found during his 1911 trip to Peru.

the Inca must have used for their roofs. The tiles are like the ones the Spanish conquerors put on their buildings. Bingham decides that the Inca lived here after the Spanish invaded Cuzco. This is the second city he was looking for—Vilcabamba.

Within one month's time, Bingham has found three Inca settlements: Machu Picchu, Vitcos, and Vilcabamba. The Inca lived in the last two cities after the Spanish conquest of Peru. But when did they live in Machu Picchu? Bingham knows he still has a lot to learn about that magical place.

THE LEADER TAKES A BREAK

In September Bingham orders Herman Tucker and Paul Lanius to stop surveying the 73rd meridian and to go to Machu Picchu. He wants them to survey the ruins and make a map.

This photograph was taken by Herman Tucker. The ruins are barely visible underneath moss and vines.

Tucker and Lanius spend two weeks surveying the ruins. They hire a small work crew to help them clear away trees and brush. Tucker learned about mapmaking while helping Kai Hendriksen on the 73rd meridian. He and Lanius create a detailed map of Machu Picchu. It sprawls across eleven sheets of paper.

Why didn't Bingham return to Machu Picchu? After all, he has spent only an afternoon there. But he decides to go to Cuzco instead to take care of business. Bingham sells some of the mules. He also picks up the equipment he will need to climb Mount Coropuna.

Harry Foote has left Peru. He is returning to Yale to teach chemistry. Bingham travels south to a city that is closer to the mountain. There he waits until Tucker finishes surveying Machu Picchu with Lanius. When Tucker joins Bingham, Lanius will head back to Connecticut.

While he waits, Bingham decides to visit an observatory in the area. It is owned by Harvard University. But he doesn't go to look at the sky through a telescope. He thinks his fellow Americans might have some news about Annie Peck. Sure enough, someone shows him an article from a U.S. newspaper. Annie Peck has climbed two eastern peaks of Mount Coropuna.

According to the newspaper, the mountain is between 18,000 and 20,000 feet (5,486 and 6,096 m) high. Bingham knows it is higher. He hopes that Peck climbed the lowest peaks and did not reach the true summit.

CLIMBING COROPUNA

Bingham and Tucker approach the mountain on October 10, 1911. They have a new military escort, Corporal Gamarra. Isaiah Bowman was supposed to join them for the climb. But he and Hendriksen are still surveying the 73rd meridian. Instead, the director of a local school joins them.

Bingham and Tucker study the mountain from a distance. They believe that the western peak is the highest. But they are not positive. The northern peak is farther away and harder to see. It's clear that neither of the two eastern summits that Annie Peck climbed is the highest one. They decide to climb the western peak.

Bingham, Tucker, the corporal, and the school director begin the climb on October 13. Within a day, they are all feeling sick. As they climb higher on the mountain, the air pressure becomes lower and the air has less oxygen. Their bodies are not used to these conditions. They have headaches, and they feel nauseated.

Bingham has packed two barometers to measure the air pressure. At the summit, the barometer will help Bingham

"The view from the top was desolate in the extreme. We were in the midst of a great volcanic desert dotted with isolated peaks covered with snow and occasional glaciers. Not an atom of green was seen anywhere. Apparently we were on top of a dead world."

—Hiram Bingham, 1922

Herman Tucker took this photograph of Hiram Bingham (right) and two of his climbing companions at the top of Mt. Coropuna.

calculate the height of the mountain peak. The lower the air pressure, the higher the peak.

On October 15, the four mountain climbers reach the top of the western peak. The summit of the extinct volcano is bleak and bare. They take two readings with their barometers. One registers 21,525 feet (6,561 m), and the other registers 22,550 feet (6,873 m). The men hope their barometers are wrong. They know of another mountain peak in the Andes that has been measured at 22,763 feet (6,938 m).

Later, Hendriksen calculates that the western peak of the mountain is 21,703 feet (6,615 m) above sea level. Bingham is sorry that Coropuna isn't the tallest mountain in the Andes. Still, it is a very tall mountain. And he is pleased that he and his companions were the first ones to climb one of the Andes' tallest peaks. They leave a U.S. flag and a Yale University flag on the summit.

HEADING HOME

Hendriksen needs another six weeks to finish his work along the 73rd meridian. The work is very difficult. The men suffer from mountain sickness while crossing the Andes. Erving decides to quit and go home.

Bowman quits as well. He arranges to meet his fellow expedition members in the city of Lima.

Hendriksen refuses to give up. Fortunately, Bingham finds him another assistant. Before Hendriksen reaches the Pacific Ocean, though, he must cross a desert. Sandstorms and intense heat make his survey work difficult. On November 23, he is thrilled to finally see the Pacific Ocean. The survey of the 73rd meridian is finished.

Bingham, Tucker, Hendriksen, and Bowman leave Peru from Lima. Bingham arrives home just before Christmas. The Yale Peruvian Expedition has achieved its main goals: They have surveyed the 73rd meridian in southern Peru. They have become the first to climb one of the tallest peaks on Mount Coropuna. And they found Vitcos and Vilcabamba. Finally, they discovered the beautiful, mysterious ruins of Machu Picchu. They made one other unexpected find: the bones that Bingham found sticking out of the gravel bank. He is eager to find out exactly how old they really are. He calls them the Cuzco bones.

"The superior character of the stone work, the presence of these splendid edifices [buildings], and of what appeared to be an unusually large number of finely constructed stone dwellings, led me to believe that Machu Picchu might prove to be the largest and most important ruin discovered in South America since the days of the Spanish conquest."

—Hiram Bingham, 1913

Meanwhile, there is a holiday to celebrate. On Christmas morning, Bingham puts on a Santa Claus costume and walks down the family's big staircase. His youngest sons think he truly is Santa Claus. They have not spent much time with their father during the past year. So they don't recognize him very easily.

These stone steps lead toward two temples. Hiram Bingham and his team first found

CHAPTER four

BACK TO PERU

In February 1912, Hiram Bingham gives a talk about his recent expedition to Peru. He speaks at the National Geographic Society, in Washington, D.C. This organization is very interested in exploration. It also publishes *National Geographic* magazine.

Bingham's talk impresses the director of the organization. The director makes Bingham a tempting offer. The National Geographic Society will give him ten thousand dollars for another expedition to Peru. The society wants Bingham to explore and map more of southern Peru. In exchange, Bingham will persuade Yale University to contribute an equal amount of money. He will also write an article for *National Geographic* magazine about the new expedition.

Bingham can't resist another chance to explore Peru. He convinces Yale University to contribute another ten thousand dollars for the expedition. The university wants Bingham to continue excavating the ruins he found on his last trip. He and other experts at Yale will want to study any bones and artifacts that he finds. And Yale would like to display these finds at its Peabody Museum of Natural History.

One problem looms. Peruvians want to keep their archaeological treasures in their own country. The laws in Peru will make it very difficult to bring anything that Bingham excavates back to the United States.

Who's Who on the 1912 Expedition

Hiram Bingham	expedition leader
Paul Bestor	assistant
Albert Bumstead	chief topographer
George Eaton	bones expert
Ellwood Erdis	engineer
Herbert Gregory	geologist
Osgood Hardy	assistant
Kenneth Heald	assistant topographer
Joseph Little	assistant
Luther Nelson	medical doctor
Robert Stephenson	assistant topographer

By spring Bingham has put together a new expedition team. No one else from the previous trip wants to return to Peru so soon. This time ten different men sign up. Herbert Gregory, a professor of geology at Yale wants to go. So does George Eaton, a curator at the Peabody Museum. Eaton is the specialist who examined the Cuzco bones. A chief topographer will also be going to Peru. He will have two assistants. Bingham has also found an engineer, a doctor, and three general assistants. Their official name is the Peruvian Expedition of 1912, under the Auspices [support] of Yale University and the National Geographic Society.

ARE THE CUZCO BONES TRULY ANCIENT?

Bingham, Eaton, and the two assistant topographers leave New York on May 16, 1912. Almost everyone else plans to arrive in three weeks. When they reach Cuzco, Eaton wants to do some unusual research. He has not figured out how old the Cuzco bones are. The ribs on the animal Bingham found were very large. Bingham hoped the animal was an ancient bison. Eaton wants to look at the ribs of modern cattle in southern Peru. Maybe they have big ribs too.

How can Eaton get a look at modern Peruvian cow ribs? He buys some beef rib bones from a butcher shop. Sure enough, they are very large. Eaton concludes that the animal bones Bingham found belonged to a modern Peruvian ox, not a bison. He is sure they are not even one thousand years old. The human bones lay right near the animal bones. So maybe the human bones are not ancient either. The bones expert collects other skeletons from gravel banks in the Cuzco region.

Herbert Gregory arrives with the second group of expedition members. The geology professor examines the gravel bank where Bingham found the bones. The professor looks at other gravel banks near Cuzco. And he looks at the bones that Eaton has collected. He decides that the gravel is from a time when glaciers covered Peru. The gravel is tens of thousands of years old. But he has bad news for Bingham: Gregory believes that all the bones that lay in the gravel are much younger than the gravel itself. The professor says people in the region have moved the gravel over the centuries. The Inca used gravel to make terraces, for example. Later, other people destroyed the terraces. That's how old gravel has come to cover up more modern bones. Bingham's Cuzco bones do not prove that humans arrived in South America thirty thousand years ago.

A team of oxen plows a field near the Andes Mountains in Peru in 2002. Modern cattle in Peru have large bones, as George Eaton learned when he studied the bones Hiram Bingham found near Cuzco in 1911.

GETTING READY FOR WORK AT MACHU PICCHU

The expedition leader hopes that the ruins of Machu Picchu will be more significant than the Cuzco bones. He wants to see the houses and temples when trees are not strangling them. And he wonders whether the expedition members will find the skeletons of Inca who were buried there. Then maybe they can figure out who lived at Machu Picchu and why. But tree removal will have to wait. Excavation will wait too.

First, the expedition team needs to make two improvements before they can work at Machu Picchu. The bridge over the Urubamba River has washed away. Bingham had crawled across that bridge during the last expedition. This time, the team will build a sturdier bridge.

Bingham knows that they also need to make a good trail from the new bridge to the ruins. The expedition members and their helpers will be carrying heavy loads up and down the trail. Any trail that they make will be too steep for mules. So men will be carrying food boxes, tents, and equipment up the trail. The boxes weigh 60 pounds (27 kilograms)! Bingham hopes they will also be carrying boxes of bones and artifacts down the trail.

Bingham asks Kenneth Heald to take charge of creating the new bridge and path. Heald is one of the assistant topographers. He is helped by ten local workers and a Peruvian soldier, Lieutenant Tomás Sotomayor.

Heald and his crew reach the Urubamba River in early July. The river is about 80 feet (24 m) wide where they will build the bridge. Large boulders stick out of the water. The boulders divide the river into four rushing streams. The men will build their bridge in four parts to connect one boulder with the next. One part will have to be 40 feet (12

"Between . . . Machu Picchu and the world that we know lie miles of breakneck trails, miles of slippery going through forests, up and down sheer mountainsides, above roaring torrents [of water]."
—*New York Times,* 1913

Hiram Bingham took this photograph of the new bridge across the Urubamba River designed by assistant topographer Kenneth Heald.

m) long. To make the bridge, they cut down some trees along the shore. Then they lash the logs together with rope so they will span the water.

It takes the men a day and a half to build the new bridge. Then they begin blazing a trail to Machu Picchu. The thick jungle growth slows them down. Heald tries starting a small fire to clear the vegetation. That doesn't help much.

Sometimes the land is too steep. Instead of blazing a straight trail, Heald decides to put some zigzags in the path. They will make the climb easier for men carrying heavy loads.

On the second day, some workers decide to start a fire to clear the trail. Heald and Sotomayor are uphill from the fire, which begins roaring in their direction. The two men run downhill through the jungle and escape the flames. While running, they both take nasty falls.

"In a minute it had gained headway and was up roaring towards us, the flames reaching 15 or 20 feet [5 or 6 m] into the air. There was nothing to be done but run, and we did that, tearing through the jungle down hill in an effort to get around the side of the fire. Suddenly, on one of my jumps, I didn't stop when I expected to, but kept right on through the air. In a minute there came a thump, and Tomás [Sotomayor] landed beside me. It amused me so much to watch him that I forgot all about my own jolted bones."

—Kenneth Heald, describing his escape from a fire set to clear a trail, 1912

Hiram Bingham took this photograph of the fire that was set during the clearing of the jungle in August 1912.

THE EXCAVATIONS BEGIN

Three days later, Bingham and Eaton climb the new trail to Machu Picchu. Ellwood Erdis comes with them. He is the expedition's engineer. Bingham, Eaton, and Erdis want to begin excavating around some of the buildings at Machu Picchu. They will look for skeletons and artifacts. Did the Inca leave pottery behind? Maybe they left jewelry or other precious objects.

Bingham decides they will dig around the temples first. They find pieces of pottery outside the walls of the Principal Temple. But they don't turn up anything inside the walls. Bingham, Eaton, Erdis, and the local workers dig for hours. They dig at least 3 feet (1 m) below the floor of the temple. In some places, they go down to 9 feet (3 m).

Next, the men try the Temple of the Three Windows. They find nothing inside. But on a terrace below the temple, they have better luck. The men uncover pieces of decorated pottery. Bingham wonders whether the Inca threw pottery out the windows of the temple. He does not consider the pottery to be very special.

Bingham was hoping to find tombs where the Inca buried dead people. He knows that the Inca buried the dead with some objects that belonged to them. And he knows these objects and the skeletons of the Inca will interest scholars. He thinks the workers need some inspiration. So he decides to offer workers rewards for finding burial sites.

This view of Machu Picchu from above shows the ancient buildings that make up what Hiram Bingham called the King's Group. Houses in this area of the city have steep roofs.

CHAPTER five

THE SEARCH FOR MORE RUINS

Bingham decides to give the workers more freedom. They want to find some burial caves so they can collect their rewards. So he decides to let them follow their instincts.

On the first day of the new system, some workers still have no luck. These men come from Cuzco. They do not know where to look for burial caves in Machu Picchu. One accidentally cuts open his toe with a sharp tool.

The local workers do much better. They find eight burial caves in one day. They find more caves during the next two weeks.

Eaton treats every burial cave with care. First, he photographs the entrance. Then he removes the bones and any objects in the cave. He also draws diagrams. These show where Eaton found a bone or an object, such as pottery.

In some caves, Eaton finds complete skeletons. In others he sees only pieces of bones. After studying many burial caves, Eaton learns something about Inca burial customs. At Machu Picchu, the Inca often buried a dead person with the knees raised. The person seemed to be sitting.

The Burial Caves

Bingham calls the burial sites at Machu Picchu caves. But often they are just large openings under big boulders. The Inca often built simple walls to seal the openings. They hoped the walls would keep away animals and strangers.

Hiram Bingham took this photograph of the first skeleton found at Machu Picchu.

Eaton finds some pottery in excellent condition. But most of the pottery he finds is in pieces. They are from the jugs, bowls, and pots that the Inca used centuries ago. Later, Eaton hopes that he and other experts at Yale's Peabody Museum will be able to put many of the pieces of pottery back together. Meanwhile, he packs everything carefully. Bingham and Eaton plan to bring crates filled with these objects home with them. But first, Bingham must get permission from the Peruvian government to remove them from Peru.

While some workers look for caves, others clear away trees and thick vegetation. Many structures are hidden by the wild jungle growth. Bingham knows that months of slow work lie ahead.

"As little by little the luxuriant jungle was hewn [cut] away and the layers of earth shoveled from around the protruding portions of the ruins, massive structures began to appear, rivaling in size and architectural skill anything ever found in Peru."

—*New York Times*, 1913

Hiram Bingham took this photograph of the ruins of Machu Picchu as the team worked to clear away the vegetation. The temple area is shown in the foreground.

At times about forty men work at Machu Picchu.

Bingham has promised the National Geographic Society that he will try to find more ruins. He has been at Machu Picchu for two weeks. With everything under control, he gets ready to leave. Bingham loves to explore. He happily leaves the slow, careful work at Machu Picchu to others.

While Bingham is off exploring new places, another team from the expedition will be working in the wilderness too. They will be working along the 73rd meridian. The team will add more details to the survey that Kai Hendriksen made in 1911. And they will create new maps of the region.

STRANDED IN THE WILDERNESS

Bingham wants to look for ruins in the wilderness between two rivers: the Urubamba and the Apurímac. The Urubamba River runs below Machu Picchu. The Apurímac runs south of the Urubamba. Bingham travels with Luis, a mule driver.

The expedition leader asks a wealthy landowner in the region if he knows of any ruins. The answer is most definitely yes. The landowner knows of three groups of ruins. He sends three local men to guide and help Bingham and Luis. The local men do not want to go on this trip. But the landowner owns their land. They pay him some of their rent by performing services for him.

Bingham and his local helpers ride on mules. Luis leads the pack mule, which carries the supplies. At the end of the day, they arrive at a ridge with some simple ruins.

The expedition leader notices about a dozen buildings. Hundreds of years ago, the Inca built them with stones and mud. Bingham follows his usual procedure. He takes photos and measures the buildings.

The landowner had told Bingham he would find the second ruins a few hours away. On the second day of the trip, the men head for these ruins. The trail takes them through very dense jungle growth. The pack mule falls down several times. The men unload the mule and carry the supplies themselves. The men have to push and pull the mules. The mules don't like the rough trail.

In the evening, the group sets up camp near a small spring, where they can get water to drink. They are on the side of a mountain about 15,000 feet (4,572 m) above sea level.

LLACTAPATA

The next day, they find the second ruins, a place called Llactapata. To get there, they travel downhill to the bottom of a valley. Bingham sees five houses arranged around a courtyard. He also notices some houses that the Inca began building but did not finish. Bingham swats away tiny flies while he measures and maps the ruins. The group stays at the ruins overnight.

In the morning, Bingham is more than ready to leave. He wants to find the third ruins. But the local men protest. They point out that it's Sunday. They say they want to rest. Bingham agrees to wait.

On Monday morning, Bingham and Luis discover that they are alone. The local men have deserted Bingham and Luis and their three mules. The two men wonder how they will find their way back. They are in a maze

This photograph by Hiram Bingham shows the ruins he found at Llactapata in 1912.

of snowy mountain peaks and deep canyons. Luckily, they meet a boy who lives in a hut near the ruins.

Bingham offers the boy a reward if he will help them find their way out of the wilderness. He has some trouble communicating with the boy, however. The boy speaks Quechua. Bingham and Luis speak Spanish.

The boy seems to understand. He leads them down a trail. They make their way very slowly. Granite boulders clog the trail. Bingham guesses that during a recent avalanche, the boulders slid off the side of a nearby mountain.

As the two men and the boy climb out of the valley, Bingham looks around in awe. Ten glaciers surround them. Eight lie in the distance in front of them, and two are behind. The boy does not know the names of the glaciers. Maybe they have no names. Bingham gives names to them

The Glaciers of Peru

The glaciers in the Andes Mountains of Peru formed about 600 million years ago. Scientists call them tropical glaciers. That's because Peru is a tropical country with a warm and wet climate. But high in the mountains, where the air is very cold, snow and ice are common. The Quelccaya Ice Cap in Peru is the largest tropical glacier in the world. It covers more than 20 square miles (52 sq. km).

all. He calls one of them the Alfreda Mitchell Glacier, in honor of his wife. He names the Taft Glacier after the president of the United States, William Howard Taft. He names another for Yale.

Bingham and his companions eventually manage to find the third group of ruins. He notices that the Inca had straightened out a crooked streambed. Then they enclosed it in a channel lined with stones. Bingham guesses that the stream

Hiram Bingham took this photograph of the glaciers he saw while looking for more ancient Inca ruins in 1912.

had wandered through the land where the Inca grew vegetables. The Inca probably straightened out the stream so they would have more agricultural land. Soon after they visit the ruins, Bingham finds the road to Cuzco.

Bingham has had an exciting trip. But he has not found any ruins that compare with Machu Picchu. He thinks the structures that he just saw weren't built with great skill by the Inca. And none of the three ruins was nearly as large as Machu Picchu.

In early September, Bingham makes one more trip into the wilderness. This time he travels over the Vilcabamba Mountains northwest of Machu Picchu. But he does not find anything special. At the end of the trip, he learns that he must travel to the capital city of Lima.

TROUBLE WITH THE GOVERNMENT

Peru's new president does not want Bingham to send any bones or artifacts from Inca ruins back to the United States. When Bingham arrives in Lima, he meets with the new president. He also visits every government official who may be able to help him. The expedition leader is as charming as he can be. And he does not give up.

After several weeks, the Peruvian government gives in to some of Bingham's demands. The government gives Bingham permission to ship the objects he finds to the United States. But the government insists that Bingham cannot begin any new excavations. And his expedition must stop excavating in Machu Picchu by December 10.

The ancient ruins of Machu Picchu seen from the top of nearby Mount Huayna Picchu.
Huayna Picchu is the mountain most often seen behind Machu Picchu in photographs.

CHAPTER six

MACHU PICCHU IN ALL ITS GLORY

Expedition members and workers have been clearing trees and vegetation for four months. When Bingham returns to Machu Picchu, he sees it in all its glory. The city looks as if the Inca carved it out of the mountain ridge. Bingham looks at every building, stairway, and terrace. Often he looks through the eye of his camera. He shoots hundreds of pictures of this small and magnificent city.

STAIRWAYS AND FOUNTAINS

Bingham notices that the Inca built many stairways to get around Machu Picchu. He counts more than one hundred. Most are on the city's streets. Others connect agricultural terraces. The stairways vary in size. Some have 150 steps or even more. Others have just 3 or

This modern photograph shows a steep staircase that leads up the ridge next to the terraces.

4 steps. One small stairway catches Bingham's eye. Inca stoneworkers had carved the stairs and railings out of one boulder.

Bingham thinks the longest stairway is the main one. It has an unusual feature. He sees about fifteen fountains on the stairway. Each one has a basin about 2.5 feet (76 cm) wide and 6 inches (15 cm) deep. The Inca drilled a hole in each basin so the water would flow in. But where did the water come from?

About 1 mile (1.6 km) from the fountains, some expedition members have found some springs on the north slope of Machu Picchu Mountain. The springs are small streams of water that flow naturally out of the earth. The Inca built a channel lined with stones to move the water to the fountains. The channel runs under a stone wall. Then it runs along a terrace and connects with the fountains.

The local people call the fountains baths. But Bingham thinks the Inca filled their water jugs at the fountains. He doesn't believe that they bathed in them.

Master Engineers

When the Inca built Machu Picchu in the 1500s, it rained about 79 inches (201 cm) every year. That is a lot of rain. The land slopes steeply. Rain running downhill would have quickly worn away the soil. Water running off the roofs of houses could have washed away soil too. Luckily, the Inca were excellent engineers. They designed the city so that rainwater and water used for drinking and bathing would drain well. The Main Drain was a ribbon of land with a stone wall on each side. It ran between the buildings and the terraces. It directed the water out of the city and into the rain forest below Machu Picchu.

The Inca also built their agricultural terraces so that they would not become soaked with water. Below the soil, they put down a layer of stones and stone chips to help drain away water. If the Inca had not been such good engineers, the buildings at Machu Picchu might have crumbled and terraces might have collapsed from the weight of the water.

This modern image shows a drain at Machu Picchu. The drains carry water away from the city.

HOUSES FIT FOR A KING

Bingham studies the houses at Machu Picchu. Most of the houses have only one room. The houses are arranged into fourteen groups. Each group seems a little different.

In one group, the Inca lined the insides of the houses with red clay. Traces of the clay still remain. Another group is built around private, terraced gardens. The only way a person could reach the gardens was by walking through one of the houses. In still another group, Bingham notices unusual details on the houses. The roofs are very steep. And the support beam over each door is an unusually large stone block. Bingham believes each group of houses belonged to a different clan, or group of related families.

This photograph by Hiram Bingham shows the details inside one of the houses at Machu Picchu. The houses had niches built into the walls. The walls were made with stone blocks perfectly fit together.

The expedition leader gives the groups of houses names. He calls the group with steep roofs the King's Group. The Inca builders set this group apart from the rest. And they chose white granite of a very high quality for the walls of the houses.

The Inca built a very useful feature into their houses. They made niches, or cavities, in the walls. Each niche is about 2 feet (61 cm) high and more than 1 foot (30 cm) wide. Bingham thinks the Inca used the niches in a number of ways. They probably stored clothing and other things in the niches. Maybe they used bottoms of empty niches as tables.

The builders placed many of the houses on terraces. Those who lived in these houses were lucky. When they looked out the windows, they saw beautiful views of the mountains.

THE LEGEND OF TAMPUTOCCO

Bingham spends time at the Sacred Plaza above the houses. This is Bingham's name for the open area where the Inca built the Principal Temple and the Temple of the Three Windows.

The Temple of the Three Windows fascinates Bingham. The windows seem too large for Machu Picchu's cool climate. They remind Bingham of a story he has read about the beginning of the Inca Empire. The story appears in several of the Spanish chronicles, written in the 1500s.

The story begins thousands of years ago, when aggressive tribes invaded Peru from the south. The native people found a refuge in a place called Tamputocco. Over a long period, this group of native people grew larger and larger. They began to occupy the land that surrounds Tamputocco.

> "The Incas were, undeniably, lovers of beautiful scenery. Many of the ruins of their most important places are located on hill tops, ridges, and mountain shoulders, from which particularly beautiful views can be obtained."
>
> —Hiram Bingham, 1913

This modern image shows the Temple of the Three Windows from below. In the foreground are terraces for growing crops.

According to the story, this is how the Inca Empire began. The Inca told the Spanish writers that Tamputocco had a hill with three windows.

Bingham thinks the Temple of the Three Windows may be the only Inca building with three large windows. He also believes that Machu Picchu makes a perfect refuge. The Inca could have easily defended their city against any attackers. In places with no steep cliffs, the Inca at Machu Picchu built high walls. For these reasons, Bingham thinks Machu Picchu is Tamputocco.

BRONZE AND BONE

Bingham takes about seven hundred photographs while he is in Peru. Most of the photos capture Machu Picchu's grand architecture. Eaton photographs smaller objects.

An Inca craftsperson made this bronze knife between A.D. 1470 and 1530. A gold bird is carved on the handle.

Eaton and his helpers find more than one hundred graves. Eaton supervises the excavations and photographs the bones and artifacts. Most of the objects are skeletons, bones, and pieces of pottery. But the Inca at Machu Picchu also made knives, pins, and other objects out of bronze.

Eaton finds some treasures. At the top of a bronze knife, an Inca metalworker made a boy and a fish. The boy is lying on his stomach. He is playing tug-of-war with the fish, which is at the end of a bronze rope. On top of another knife sits a llama. A hummingbird with a long beak decorates the top of a pin. To create each work of art, a skilled metalworker poured hot liquid metal into a mold, made especially for the knife or pin.

On December 1, Bingham sails from Lima with other expedition members. He also travels with his photos and one hundred cases of bones and artifacts. His wife, Alfreda, and his two oldest sons meet him in Panama. They have not seen him in almost six months, and they want to escort him home.

BINGHAM SPREADS THE NEWS

When Bingham first arrives home before Christmas, he does not feel like a successful explorer. He has not found a new Inca city on this trip. And he has not climbed to the top of a tall mountain peak, where no one has been before. To make matters worse, a New Haven, Connecticut, newspaper has published a story about the boy who rescued him in the wilderness. Bingham thinks the story makes him look silly and helpless.

Bingham goes to the National Geographic Society soon after his arrival. He shows his best photos to the editor of the society's magazine. Most of

them are of Machu Picchu. The editor thinks the photographs are wonderful. Bingham's account of the expedition impresses the editor too. He decides to devote an entire issue of *National Geographic* magazine to Bingham's expedition. Bingham will write the article and provide the pictures.

The story of Bingham's expedition appears in *National Geographic* the following April (1913). In the article, Bingham discusses the significance of Machu Picchu. He mentions the size of the ruins and the many structures that expedition members have uncovered. The explorer also emphasizes that the Spanish never lived there. So they did not change the appearance of the city.

Bingham is beginning to truly appreciate the value of his discovery. Two months after his article appears, a New York City newspaper publishes a front-page story about Machu Picchu. The newspaper leaves no doubts in the reader's mind about Bingham's achievement. A heading inside the article says it all: "Prof. Hiram Bingham of Yale Makes the Greatest Archaeological Discovery of the Age by Locating and Excavating Ruins of Machu Picchu on a Peak of the Andes Mountains."

The media lavished attention on Hiram Bingham after his discovery and excavation of the ancient ruins at Machu Picchu (shown here).

The zigzag trail leading up the mountain to the ancient ruins can be seen on the left in this photograph taken from above Machu Picchu.

EPILOGUE

Only a few local people knew about Machu Picchu in 1911. Hiram Bingham told the world about this beautiful Inca city perched on a ridge in the Andes Mountains. And people from around the world have been coming to see it ever since.

Machu Picchu has become one of the best-known archaeological sites in the Western Hemisphere. In 1983 the United Nations Educational, Scientific, and Cultural Organization declared it to be a World Heritage Site. In 2006 more than four hundred thousand people visited Machu Picchu. Many of them went home with a true appreciation for the great Inca builders who created the city centuries ago.

Modern experts agree that the Inca built Machu Picchu when Pachacuti ruled the Inca Empire (1438–1471). But why did the Inca build it? Many experts believe that the small city was one of Pachacuti's royal estates. The weather is warmer in Machu Picchu than in Cuzco. Experts think that Pachacuti stayed there in the winter to enjoy the higher temperatures. He probably brought the royal family and other important Inca to stay with him at his estate. It is likely that Pachacuti stayed in one of the houses in the King's Group. Bingham labeled those houses correctly.

Tourists stand on top of the terraces at Machu Picchu. Hundreds of thousands of tourists visit the Inca ruins each year.

Machu Picchu also had a year-round population. The people who planted crops for Pachacuti and did other work lived there all year. The graves that Bingham's expedition found probably belonged to these

Returning Peru's Treasure

The people of Peru are very proud of Machu Picchu. Some feel strongly that the pottery, bronze objects, and skeletons that Bingham brought to Yale University in 1912 do not belong in the United States. They want to see the objects displayed near Machu Picchu.

In the early 2000s, the government of Peru demanded that Yale return the objects. Seven years later, the university agreed to return most of them. Yale and the government of Peru will organize a traveling museum show with objects from Machu Picchu. Earnings from this show will help build a new research center and museum in Cuzco. The objects will be on display in the new museum.

Artifacts from Machu Picchu such as pottery (right) and tools (below) are displayed at Yale's Peabody Museum in 2006.

Modern scholars believe that royal family members were buried in Cuzco.

When Bingham tried to analyze Machu Picchu, he made some mistakes. He thought Machu Picchu was Tamputocco, the birthplace of the Inca Empire. Scholars think Machu Picchu is not old enough to be the Inca's birthplace.

It is easy to understand why Bingham did not get everything right. He was a talented explorer, not an archaeologist. Bingham loved the thrill of discovery. He pushed mules up steep trails. He hiked in the rain. Sometimes mosquitoes made a meal of him. When he found a new and important place, he forgot all about his suffering. His greatest achievement was bringing Machu Picchu to the attention of the world.

MACHU PICCHU ARCHAEOLOGICAL SITE

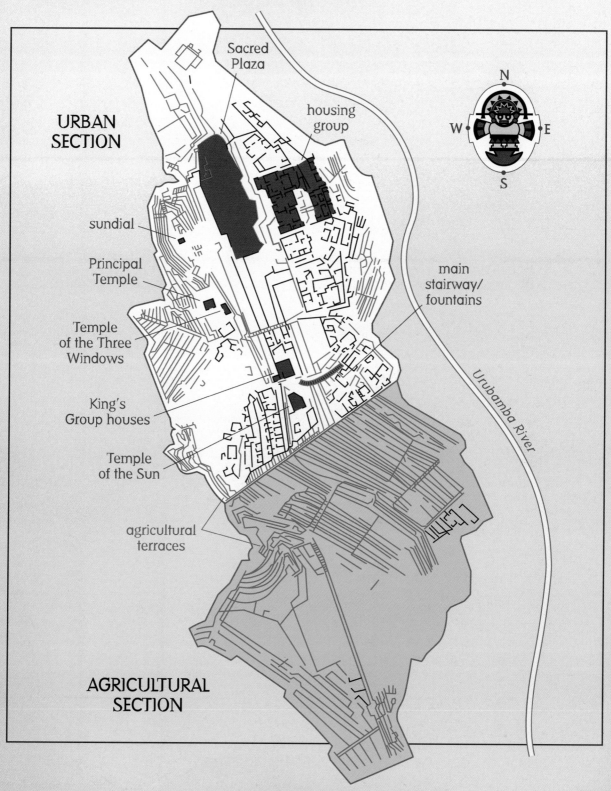

URBAN
SECTION

Sacred
Plaza

housing
group

N
W ● E
S

sundial

Principal
Temple

main
stairway/
fountains

Temple
of the Three
Windows

Urubamba River

King's
Group houses

Temple
of the Sun

agricultural
terraces

AGRICULTURAL
SECTION

TIMELINE

1438–1471
Pachacuti rules the Inca Empire. The Inca build the city of Machu Picchu during his reign.

1532
The Spanish conqueror Francisco Pizarro invades Peru.

1572
The Spanish execute Tupac Amarú, the last Inca ruler. The execution marks the end of the Inca Empire.

1821
Peru wins independence from Spain.

1911
Hiram Bingham III finds Machu Picchu on a ridge northwest of Cuzco.

Bingham finds the ruins of Vitcos and Vilcabamba, cities where the last Inca rulers lived.

Bingham's expedition maps the 73rd meridian in Peru, from the Andes Mountains to the Pacific Ocean.

Bingham climbs the western peak of Mount Coropuna, one of the tallest mountains in the Andes.

1912
Bingham leads a new expedition to clear and excavate Machu Picchu.

Bingham finds the ruins of three more Inca cities.

1913
National Geographic magazine prints the story of Bingham's discovery of Machu Picchu.

1964
U.S. explorer Gene Savoy rediscovers Vilcabamba.

1983
UNESCO (the United Nations Educational, Scientific, and Cultural Organization) declares Machu Picchu to be a World Heritage Site.

2003

An international team of explorers rediscovers the ruins of Llactapata—one of three additional ruins that Bingham found in 1912.

2007

Yale University agrees to return most of the artifacts from Bingham's 1912 expedition to Peru. The Peruvian government will build a new museum for them in Cuzco.

PRONUNCIATION GUIDE

The language of the Inca Empire was Quechua. The language has not died out. Experts estimate that ten million people still speak Quechua in parts of Peru, Bolivia, Colombia, Ecuador, Argentina, and Chile. Along with Spanish, Quechua is an official language of Peru. Below is a pronunciation key to some of the Quechua words and names used in the text.

Apurímac	ah-poo-REE-mahk
Coropuna	koh-roh-POO-nah
Cuzco	KOO-skoh
Machu Picchu	MAH-choo PEE-choo
Pachacuti	pah-chah-KOO-tee
Quechua	KEHCH-wuh
Tamputocco	tahm-poo-TOH-koh
Tupac Amarú	too-PAHK ahm-AHR-oo
Urubamba	oo-roo-BAHM-bah
Vilcabamba	weel-kah-BAHM-bah
Vitcos	VEET-kohs

GLOSSARY

archaeologist: an expert who studies old buildings, graves, tools, and other objects to learn about past cultures and civilizations

artifact: an object made by a human being, often long ago. Archaeologists study artifacts to learn about ancient cultures.

chronicle: an account of historical events, arranged according to date

clan: a group of families who are usually related to one another

excavate: to dig up or around something that has been buried underground, such as ancient ruins

glaciers: large masses of ice that move very slowly across the land

meridians: imaginary circles around Earth that pass through the North and South poles. Mapmakers use meridians to determine east–west measurements on Earth.

ruins: the remains of a building (or another large object) that has decayed over time

survey: to measure an area for making a map

terrace: a raised, flat platform of land. In very hilly areas, a series of terraces can make farming easier.

volcano: a mountain with openings through which lava, ash, and gases erupt. An extinct volcano, such as Mount Coropuna, no longer erupts.

WHO'S WHO?

Hiram Bingham III (1875–1956) Hiram Bingham was born in Honolulu, Hawaii. His father, Hiram Bingham II, was a Protestant missionary. In this job, he worked to convert native Hawaiians to Christianity.

In his teens, Bingham attended a private boarding school in Massachusetts. He earned his undergraduate degree from Yale University in 1898. He received a doctorate degree from Harvard University in 1905. He taught South American history at Yale from 1907 to 1923.

Bingham led his first expedition to Peru in 1911. On that expedition, he found Machu Picchu. He led a second expedition to Peru in 1912. His teams spent months clearing and excavating Machu Picchu. They returned with thousands of human bones and artifacts from Inca graves.

The explorer led a third expedition to Peru in 1915. The Peruvians did not want him there. They accused him of trying to steal gold and threatened to arrest him. He left and never returned.

The United States entered World War I (1914–1918) in 1917. That year Bingham learned to fly airplanes. During the war, he commanded a flying school for pilots from the United States and its allies.

After the war, Bingham entered politics. In 1922 he was elected lieutenant governor of Connecticut (the lieutenant governor is the state's second-highest official, after the governor). He was elected to the U.S. Senate in 1925 and served until 1933. He spent many of his remaining years in business.

Bingham wrote more than a dozen books about his explorations in South America. These books include *Inca Land* (1922), *Machu Picchu, a Citadel of the Incas* (1930), and *Lost City of the Incas* (1948).

Isaiah Bowman (1878–1950) Isaiah Bowman was born in Waterloo, Ontario, Canada. As a young man, he attended Harvard University and Yale University.

Bowman taught geography at Yale from 1905 to 1915. During that time, Bowman went on three expeditions to South America, including Hiram Bingham's 1911 expedition. From 1915 to 1935, Bowman served as director of the American Geographical Society. At the end of World War I, Bowman advised U.S. president Woodrow Wilson on questions about international boundaries.

In 1935 Bowman became president of Johns Hopkins University. During World War II (1939–1945), Bowman again advised the U.S. government on boundary issues.

George Eaton (1872–1949) George Eaton was born in New Haven, Connecticut. He graduated from Yale University in 1894 and earned his Ph.D. there three years later.

In 1899 he began working at Yale's Peabody Museum. During his career, he held several positions at the museum, including curator of osteology and associate curator of vertebrate paleontology. In 1904 Eaton brought a prehistoric animal that he had restored to the world's fair in Saint Louis, Missouri. His exhibit won a gold medal for Yale.

Eaton went to Peru with Hiram Bingham on his 1912 exhibition. He continued working at the Peabody Museum until his death.

SOURCE NOTES

14 Hiram Bingham, *Inca Land* (Cambridge, MA: Riverside Press, 1922), 5–6.

20 Hiram Bingham, *Inca Land*, 314.

22 Ibid., 316.

27 Ibid., 321.

33 Hiram Bingham, *Inca Land*, 43.

35 Hiram Bingham, "In the Wonderland of Peru: The Work Accomplished by the Peruvian Expedition of 1912, under the Auspices of Yale University and the National Geographic Society," *National Geographic* 24, no. 4 (April 1913): 408.

40 *New York Times*, "Lost City in the Clouds Found after Centuries," June 15, 1913, 1.

42 Hiram Bingham, "In the Wonderland of Peru," 424.

46 *New York Times*, "Lost City in the Clouds."

57 Hiram Bingham, "In the Wonderland of Peru," 473–477.

61 *New York Times*, "Lost City in the Clouds."

64 Ibid., 453.

SELECTED BIBLIOGRAPHY

BBC. "Machu Picchu in Danger of Collapse." *BBC News*. March 8, 2001. http://news.bbc.co.uk/2/hi/americas/1208026.stm (October 30, 2007).

Bingham, Alfred M. *Portrait of an Explorer: Hiram Bingham, Discoverer of Machu Picchu*. Ames: Iowa State University Press, 1989.

Bingham, Hiram. "The Discovery of Machu Picchu." *Harper's Magazine* 126 (1913), 709–719.

———. *Inca Land*. Cambridge, MA: Riverside Press, 1922.

———. "In the Wonderland of Peru: The Work Accomplished by the Peruvian Expedition of 1912, under the Auspices of Yale University and the National Geographic Society." *National Geographic Magazine* 24, no. 4 (April 1913), 387–573.

———. *Lost City of the Incas: The Story of Machu Picchu and Its Builders*. New York: Atheneum, 1948.

Burger, Richard L., and Lucy C. Salazar, eds. *Machu Picchu: Unveiling the Mystery of the Incas*. New Haven, CT: Yale University Press, 2004.

D'Altroy, Terence N. *The Incas*. Malden, MA: Blackwell Publishers, 2002.

Horwitz, Tony. *The Devil May Care: Fifty Intrepid Americans and Their Quest for the Unknown*. New York: Oxford University Press, 2003.

Lubow, Arthur. "The Possessed." *New York Times Magazine*, June 24, 2007, 42–49, 68, 82–83.

New York Times. "Lost City in the Clouds Found after Centuries." June 15, 1913, 1.

———."Yale and Peruvian Officials Agree on Return of Artifacts. August 17, 2007, B3.

Wright, Kenneth R., and Alfredo Valencia Zegarra. *Machu Picchu: A Civil Engineering Marvel*. Reston, VA: ASCE Press, 2000.

FURTHER READING AND WEBSITES

BOOKS

Allison, Amy. *Building History: Machu Picchu*. San Diego: Lucent Books, 2003.

Calvert, Patricia. *The Ancient Inca*. Danbury, CT: Franklin Watts, 2005.

Mann, Elizabeth. *Machu Picchu: The Story of the Amazing Inkas and Their City in the Clouds*. New York: Mikaya Press, 2000.

Márquez, Herón. *Peru in Pictures*. Minneapolis: Twenty-First Century Books, 2004.

Reinhard, Johan. *Discovering the Inca Ice Maiden*. Washington, DC: National Geographic Children's Books, 1998.

Schlesinger, Arthur M., ed. *The Ancient Incas: Chronicles from National Geographic*. Philadelphia: Chelsea House, 1999.

Takacs, Stephanie. *The Inca*. Danbury, CT: Children's Press, 2005.

Wilcox, Charlotte. *Mummies, Bones, and Body Parts*. Minneapolis: Carolrhoda Books, 2001.

———. *Mummies and Their Mysteries*. Minneapolis: Carolrhoda Books, 1993.

WEBSITES

MachuPicchu360.com
http://www.mp360.com/eng/360/mp064.html
Here you can take a virtual tour of Machu Picchu. You feel like you are right there on the top of the ridge. Enjoy a close look at Inca architecture and the stunning scenery all around.

Machu Picchu: Unveiling the Mysteries of the Incas
http://www.fieldmuseum.org/machupicchu/
This site presents the highlights of a traveling exhibit about Machu Picchu. The exhibit was created by Yale University's Peabody Museum of Natural History. But you access it from the website of the Field Museum, in Chicago, Illinois, which was on the show's tour. You can see beautiful examples of Inca craftsmanship and read more about Machu Picchu.

Mummies of the Inca
http://www.pbs.org/wgbh/nova/peru
This site is a companion to a show in public television's *NOVA* series. The show was about mummies. The website describes the journey of an archaeologist to the top of a peak in the Andes Mountains in Peru. The archaeologist was looking for frozen mummies. The mummies were the remains of people whom the Inca sacrificed to their gods.

vgsbooks.com
http://www.vgsbooks.com
This site is the homepage of the Visual Geography Series®, and is updated regularly. The website offers links to all sorts of useful information, including maps and photos of Peru. The site also includes links to sites with geographical, historical, demographic, culturual, and economic websites.

INDEX

ABOUT THE AUTHOR

Deborah Kops has written more than a dozen books for children and young adults, including *Ancient Rome* and *Palenque*. She enjoys visiting historic sites in Greater Boston, Massachusetts, where she lives with her husband and son.

PHOTO ACKNOWLEDGMENTS

The images in this book are used with the permission of: © Guy Marks/Axiom Photographic Agency/Getty Images, p. 4; © iStockphoto.com/Edward Davis, p. 5; © iStockphoto.com/Maxime Vige, p. 6; © North Wind Picture Archives, p. 8 (left); The Granger Collection, New York, pp. 8 (right), 14, 29, 59; © Peter Adams/The Image Bank/Getty Images, p. 10; Library of Congress (LC-USZ62-99525), p. 11; © Paul Grogan/Alamy, p. 12; © Hiram Bingham/National Geographic Society Image Collection, Courtesy of the Peabody Museum of Natural History, Yale University, New Haven, Connecticut, pp. 17, 22, 28, 31, 32, 34, 41, 42, 46, 47, 49, 50, 54, 56; © Gina Martin/National Geographic/Getty Images, p. 18; © age fotostock/ SuperStock, p. 21; © Angelo Cavalli/SuperStock, p. 24; © Wolfgang Kaehler/ Alamy, p. 26; © Neil McAllister/Alamy, p. 27; © John & Lisa Merrill/Photographer's Choice/Getty Images, p. 36; © ullstein-Lillehaug/Peter Arnold, Inc., p. 39; © iStockphoto.com/Marshall Bruce, p. 44; © David Madison/The Image Bank/Getty Images, p. 52; © iStockphoto.com/Oscar Schnell, p. 53; © iStockphoto.com/Maria Veras, p. 55; © Travel Ink/Gallo Images/Getty Images, p. 58; © Holton Collection/ SuperStock, pp. 60-61; © iStockphoto.com/Feldore McHugh, p. 62;© John & Lisa Merrill/The Image Bank/Getty Images, p. 64; AP Photo/Bob Child, p. 65 (both). Illustrations by Laura Westlund/Independent Picture Service.

Cover: © Taxi/Getty Images